BIOGRAPHY FROM ANCIENT CIVILIZATIONS
LEGENDS, FOLKLORE, AND STORIES OF ANCIENT WORLDS

The Life and Times of

RICHARD THE LIONHEART

Mitchell Lane
PUBLISHERS

P.O. Box 196
Hockessin, Delaware 19707
www.mitchelllane.com

BIOGRAPHY FROM ANCIENT CIVILIZATIONS
LEGENDS, FOLKLORE, AND STORIES OF ANCIENT WORLDS

TITLES IN THE SERIES

The Life and Times of

Alexander the Great	Joan of Arc
Archimedes	Julius Caesar
Aristotle	King Arthur
Augustus Caesar	Leif Eriksson
Buddha	Marco Polo
Catherine the Great	Moses
Charlemagne	Nero
Cicero	Nostradamus
Cleopatra	Pericles
Confucius	Plato
Constantine	Pythagoras
Erik the Red	Rameses the Great
Genghis Khan	Richard the Lionheart
Hammurabi	Socrates
Herodotus	Thucydides
Hippocrates	William the Conqueror
Homer	

The Life and Times of

RICHARD THE LIONHEART

Susan Sales Harkins and William H. Harkins

Mitchell Lane **PUBLISHERS**

Printing   1   2   3   4   5   6   7   8   9

Library of Congress Cataloging-in-Publication Data

Harkins, Susan Sales.
 The life and times of Richard the Lionheart / by Susan Sales Harkins and William H. Harkins.
   p. cm. — (Biography from ancient civilizations)
 Includes bibliographical references and index.
 ISBN 978-1-58415-699-4 (library bound)
 1. Richard I, King of England, 1157–1199—Juvenile literature. 2. Great Britain—History—Richard I, 1189–1199—Juvenile literature. 3. Great Britain—Kings and rulers—Biography—Juvenile literature. 4. Crusades—Third, 1189–1192–Juvenile literature. I. Harkins, William H. II. Title.
 DA207.H17 2008
 942.03'2092—dc22
 [B]
                                                             2008020916

ABOUT THE AUTHORS: Susan and William Harkins live in Kentucky, where they enjoy writing together for children. Susan has written many books for adults and children. William is a history buff. In addition to writing, he is a member of the Air National Guard.

PUBLISHER'S NOTE: This story is based on the authors' extensive research, which they believe to be accurate. Documentation of such research is contained on page 46.
   The internet sites referenced herein were active as of the publication date. Due to the fleeting nature of some web sites, we cannot guarantee they will all be active when you are reading this book.
   To reflect current usage, we have chosen to use the secular era designations BCE ("before the common era") and CE ("of the common era") instead of the traditional designations BC ("before Christ") and AD (*anno Domini*, "in the year of the Lord").

PLB

BIOGRAPHY FROM
ANCIENT CIVILIZATIONS
LEGENDS, FOLKLORE, AND STORIES OF ANCIENT WORLDS

CONTENTS

Chapter 1   A Holy War......................................7
             FYInfo*: Saladin 11
Chapter 2   A Twelfth-Century Prince.............13
             FYInfo: Henry and Eleanor 19
Chapter 3   Richard, Duke of Normandy 21
             FYInfo: Philip Augustus.................27
Chapter 4   Richard the Lionheart 29
             FYInfo: Concerning Crusaders
             Who Were to Travel by Sea......35
Chapter 5   Richard I 37
             FYInfo: King John and the
             Magna Carta 42
Chapter Notes...43
Chronology 44
Timeline in History 45
Further Reading..46
    For Young Adults..46
    Works Consulted...46
    On the Internet 46
Glossary 47
Index..48
                    *For Your Information

En route to the Holy Land, King Richard's army captured the port city of Lemessus (now Limassol) on Cyprus. One traditional story says that Richard used silver chains to bind the island's king because he promised not to place him in irons. Richard later used the port to supply his army.

CHAPTER
ONE

A HOLY WAR

For the Kingdom of Jerusalem, 1185 CE was a bad year. Their able and beloved king, Baldwin the Leper, died. During his short reign, Baldwin had worked tirelessly to keep the peace between his Christian subjects and the Muslims who surrounded his kingdom.

Christians, Jews, and Muslims all claimed the holy city as their own, but Christians had ruled the Kingdom of Jerusalem since the Second Crusade. Under Christian rule, all three religious groups lived and worshiped as they pleased in the holy city. It was a tense peace, but it was peace just the same.

Grief turned to fear and disgust when Guy of Lusignan became Jerusalem's new king. He was weak and thought nothing of his subjects. His quest for war led him to Reginald (or Raynald) of Châtillon. As much as Guy loved war, Reginald hated Muslims. When Guy asked for war, Reginald led an expedition against Muslim-held Mecca and Medina (both in modern-day Saudi Arabia).

In 1186, Reginald captured a caravan and took a grand prize. The sister of the Great Salah ad-Din was in that caravan. Outraged, Salah ad-Din, called Saladin (SAL-ed-in) by Christians, called for a jihad (a holy war). He called for Muslims to fight the Christians and reclaim their holy city of Jerusalem.

Lack of water was the enemy at the Horns of Hattin. The Crusaders marched through the desert to meet Saladin's army, but they took no water with them. Saladin was smart enough to position his army between the Crusaders and Lake Tiberias.

The two armies met on the searing hot plains known as the Horns of Hattin near Lake Tiberias (the Sea of Galilee) in July 1187. The Christian army wilted in the hot sun while Saladin's army stood between them and the lake, their only source of water. The Muslims lit fires to create thick clouds of smoke.

Saladin's men were born and raised in the dry, hot air of the holy lands. They were accustomed to fighting in the heat. Saladin had the upper hand, but King Guy was confident. His army carried the True Cross. Christians believed this cross was the cross on which Jesus had been crucified. They believed an army that carried the True Cross could not be defeated. They were wrong: Saladin's Muslim army won a great victory that day.

Saladin spared King Guy, but Reginald wasn't so lucky. When Reginald refused to convert to Islam, the Muslim religion, Saladin thrust his sword through the Christian's stomach. (Some sources say

Reginald was executed for drinking water without Saladin's permission.)

A few months later, on October 2, 1187, Saladin's army entered the city of Jerusalem after a negotiated surrender. Christians and Jews with enough money bought their freedom. Everyone else became slaves to the Muslims.

When Saladin closed the city to Christian pilgrims, Christians around the world called for a new war: the Third Crusade.

Richard I, the King of England, heard the cry and took the cross, promising to march an army to the Holy Land and reclaim the kingdom of Jerusalem. By late 1191, the Great Saladin had suffered two major defeats at the hands of Richard I. Surrendering Acre (AH-kree) to the crusaders had damaged Saladin's military reputation.[1] Even so, Richard didn't let his victories go to his head. His real quest, Jerusalem, still lay ahead.

Progress was slow. Richard's army stopped many times to repair castles destroyed by Saladin's army. While camping, men searched for grass and hay to feed their horses and mules. It was dangerous work because Saladin's army was always close by.

One afternoon, an exhausted knight rode into camp, collapsed before Richard, and asked for help. A small party of knights was under attack, he reported. They were so outnumbered by the Muslims that the crusading knights had surrendered at once.

Richard gathered several other knights and rode out, hoping to rescue his men. In the distance, he saw hundreds of Muslim soldiers. His companions warned him not to ride out against such a large army. They all knew that

Statue of Richard I in Shrewsbury, England

The bloody Battle of Acre, as imagined by French illustrator Gustave Doré in the 1800s. On the Third Crusade, Richard and his knights breached the walls of Acre and defeated the Muslim army there.

Richard was the driving force behind their crusade. If he died, their crusade would die with him.

An impatient Richard shouted, "I sent those men here. If they die without me, I do not wish to be called king any longer!"[2] With that, he spurred his horse and led an attack against the Muslims, falling upon them "like a thunderbolt."[3]

Richard's attack was so fierce and sudden that the Muslim force retreated. Richard returned to camp with all the captured knights.

His heroism that day won him the devotion of his men and the admiration and respect of Saladin.[4] Just the mention of Richard's name struck such terror that for many years following the skirmish, Arab and Turkish mothers warned their children that Malek Rik (King Richard) would come for them if they didn't behave.[5]

Saladin

Saladin, Richard's foe, was a child of the crusades. His father was a general in the Muslim army commanded by Nur ad-Din.

Born a Kurd in 1137 or 1138, Yusuf ibn Ayyub Salah ad-Din, which means "Righteousness of the Faith," grew up surrounded by soldiers and their memories of the Second Crusade (1145–1149). That's when the Christian crusaders reclaimed the Kingdom of Jerusalem. After the Second Crusade, Nur ad-Din united Syria and made Damascus his capital. He surrounded the Christian-held Jerusalem, and then sent a young Saladin to seize Egypt.

Saladin, who is said to have been small and blind in one eye, was a strong diplomat with equally strong military skills. By 1172, he was master of the Muslim province of Egypt and Syria. After Nur ad-Din's death in 1174, Saladin became one of the most powerful rulers in western Asia.[6]

During Saladin's time, Christians and Muslims traded and lived peacefully in the Holy Land. Both Saladin and Baldwin the Leper, the king of Jerusalem, worked hard to maintain the peace. That peace was shattered after Baldwin's death, when Guy of Lusignan failed to control his nobles—especially Reginald of Châtillon.

Saladin's subsequent capture of Jerusalem triggered the Third Crusade. European Christians poured into the Holy Lands to free the holy city of Jerusalem. Although Saladin's men outnumbered Richard's army, Richard was the better soldier. Despite all that military power, the Third Crusade was a battle of strategy and diplomacy. Both Richard and Saladin proved worthy opponents on both accounts. Also like Richard, Saladin preferred to lead his men into battle.[7]

Saladin raises his sword in victory. According to tradition, Saladin's sword was far superior to Richard's. It could slice through silk and crush boulders.

Based on his effigy at Fontevraud Abbey, this etching probably gives us a good idea of what Richard I looked like. From writings, we know that he was tall and considered handsome.

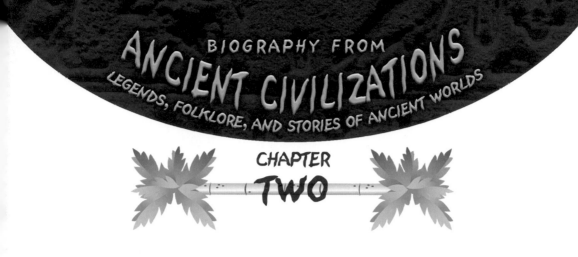

A TWELFTH-CENTURY PRINCE

Twenty years after Saladin was born in the Middle East, Eleanor of Aquitaine gave birth to an English prince. Richard was born on September 8, 1157, probably at Beaumont Palace in Oxford. Henry II and Eleanor had already known heartbreak. Their first son, William, died before Richard was born. In that era, many children did not live to adulthood. Not even the king and queen of England could escape the reality of twelfth-century life. Their second son, Henry "The Young King," was two and a half years older than Richard.

Richard's world was harsh, but it was even worse for his subjects. Rural peasants lived in small huts, which they shared with their livestock—if they were lucky enough to have any. They made their homes of stone, slate, or wood with a thatch roof. The air was heavy with the stench of human and animal waste. Babies crawled and learned to walk on hard dirt floors. A simple circle of stones on the floor marked the fireplace. Smoke stung everyone's eyes as it drifted out through the roof or windows. Wooden shutters kept out drafts and foul weather.

A man and his sons harvested crops by hand. Sometimes the mother and daughters also worked in the fields. Part of every crop went to the lord of the manor—the landlord. What was left, the family stored in a small loft. In good years, the family had enough to last until the next harvest. If the crops failed, the family would starve, maybe to death. Drought and pests were common problems.

On goods days, a son would snare a rabbit, which the mother would put in a pot with a few vegetables. After a long hard day that began with just bread and ale, even a meal of pease pudding tasted good. This "pudding" was more like a thick sauce made of boiled peas, butter, mint, a bit of whatever other vegetables were at hand—and, if the family was doing well, a hunk of bacon. Flour was used to thicken the stew. The poorer the family, the more flour and fewer vegetables were used.

Everyone slept in the hut's common room on a prickly straw mattress. In cold weather, they shivered under rough woolen blankets. Livestock spent the night in stalls, but under the same roof as the family.

In town, merchants lived above their stores and workshops. Shops and homes were small and uncomfortable. During times of famine, living in a town was hard. Not everyone had enough land to grow vegetables. If the farmers didn't have enough to go around, townsfolk paid outrageous prices or went hungry.

Life for nobles and royalty was somewhat easier. They seldom starved like peasants and laborers. However, their life was uncomfortable, at least by modern terms. Castles were drafty and damp. No one had indoor plumbing—it simply didn't exist. Royals and peasants alike got sick and died before their time.

The biggest difference between commoners and the nobility was their work. Commoners worked and nobles didn't, unless they were at war, and they were often at war. Noblemen spent their free time jousting and hunting. Women had only one real duty, and that was to produce a son to inherit her husband's land. Often, the wife managed the estate when her husband was away. The nobility seldom married for love. Most noble marriages joined two families' land and money.

Richard's England was a harsh place, but a lack of technology wasn't the only problem. Politics made life dangerous for nobles and peasants alike. Henry I, Richard's great-grandfather, died in 1135 without leaving an heir. His daughter Matilda had the best claim to the

English throne, but she was living in France, having married Geoffrey V of Anjou. (Matilda's brother William died during his teens in the *White Ship* tragedy of 1120.) Geoffrey was the son of Fulk V, the Count of Anjou and King of Jerusalem from 1131 to 1143.

Despite her claim, the English didn't like Matilda. According to a contemporary chronicler, "Few in England wanted to see Matilda seated on the vacant [throne]."[1] The English thought she was unpleasant and arrogant.

Stephen of Blois, Henry's nephew by his sister Adela, also claimed the throne. The king had been fond of Stephen and raised him after his father died. Henry gave Stephen estates in both England and Normandy, and by 1130, Stephen was the richest man in the kingdom. After Henry's death, Stephen seized the royal treasury and the throne. On December 22, 1135, the citizens of London crowned Stephen king. Matilda was displeased, to say the least.

Stephen was a good man, but not a very strong king. He was unable to control his rowdy barons.

In 1139, Robert of Gloucester (Matilda's half brother) invaded England on Matilda's behalf, throwing the country into civil war. Battle followed battle, and England's barons switched loyalties. For a short time, Matilda's troops took control and named her queen, but she didn't last. The citizens ran her out of London.

In 1153, Matilda's son, Henry of Anjou, took up his mother's cause. A compromise ended the war. Stephen would rule until his death, and the throne would pass to Henry, who didn't have to wait long. Stephen died the next year, in 1154. As promised, the throne passed to the very French Henry II, also known as Henry Plantagenet (and Richard's father).

At birth, the royal couple entrusted Richard to a wet-nurse named Hodierna. The boy spent his first five years with her and not his family. After all, Henry and Eleanor had a kingdom to run. It was common during those days for nurses to raise noble offspring. Most likely, Richard was very fond of Hodierna. As king, he gave her a large pension.

Around the age of five, Richard began his education. He studied Latin, mathematics, geometry, music, and astronomy. He also trained for war. Fencing, wrestling, running, throwing a javelin, and horseback riding were part of his everyday lessons.

Richard was eleven when his parents arranged a marriage to Alice, the daughter of Louis VII, the king of France. Three years later, at the age of fourteen, he inherited Aquitaine from his mother, which made him the duke of Aquitaine. Around the same time, Henry II made his oldest son, Henry, king of England, duke of Normandy, and

Plantagenet Family Tree   *Capetian Family Tree*
(England and Normandy)   *(France)*

William the Conqueror   Philip I

Adela   Henry I — Matilda of Scotland   Louis VI

Matilda — Geoffrey V Plantagenet of Anjou

Stephen of Blois   Henry II — Eleanor of Aquitaine — Louis VII

Henry III — Margaret

Richard I   Alice

Geoffrey VI   Philip II

Joan

John
(Lackland)

Richard was descended from William the Conqueror, a Norman knight who conquered England in 1066. Richard's family, called the Plantagenets, was closely connected to the Capetian line of French kings.

count of Poitou. He intended to share his kingdom with the boy until he died. Geoffrey, who was a year younger than Richard, was betrothed to Constance, the heiress of Brittany (in France). Through his wife, Geoffrey would be the duke of Brittany.

Because of their French alliances, Henry II's three older sons had to pay homage to Louis VII of France, the dukedom's overlord and, interestingly, their mother's ex-husband. The law gave Louis the higher claim on their allegiance.

Paying homage to the French king put Henry's sons in an odd situation. Throughout his life, Louis did his best to destroy the Plantagenet hold on France that began with Henry II. Technically, Henry II was a feudal vassal of the king of France, meaning he pledged loyalty to the king, who in turn provided Henry with land. However, Henry owned more territory and was more powerful than the French king.

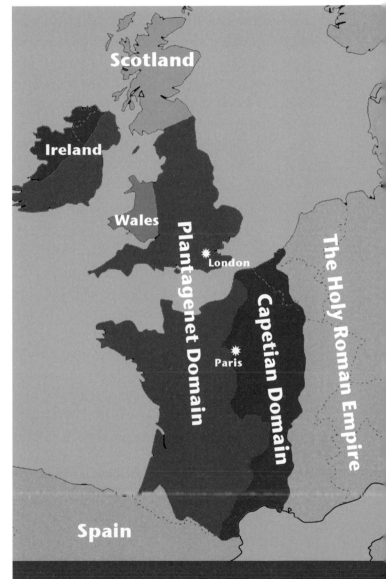

Henry II ruled England and a large part of France (blue). He had to answer to King Louis VII, who owned much less land (red).

Several times Louis incited Henry's sons to rebel against their father. Louis might not have had the military power to subdue the Plantagenets, but he could help them destroy themselves.

A good example of Louis' interference occurred just before Richard turned sixteen. All of the boys were already annoyed with their father because their titles were in name only. Henry II kept a tight rein on government, allowing none of the boys to rule their holdings. He wanted his sons to serve while he maintained overall control of their kingdom. His plan only alienated his eager sons.

Henry and Eleanor's youngest son, John, had no claim to any land, which earned him the nickname of John Lackland. Henry decided to give the boy some of the land he'd already given to his son Henry.

When young Henry complained to his mother, she sent him to Louis. Her advice isn't as odd as it might seem. Louis VII was now young Henry's father-in-law, since Henry had married Louis' daughter Margaret. (The young couple had one son, who died as an infant.)

When young Henry fled to King Louis, Henry II prepared for war. Louis was happy to help drive a wedge between father and son, and he also advised war. Richard and Geoffrey joined their brother Henry and King Louis in the fight against their father. When Eleanor tried to join them at Louis' court, she was arrested and sent home to Henry II. He promptly locked her away in a well-guarded castle.

History puts most of the blame for the rebellion on Eleanor and Henry II, and not on their sons, even though the boys were eager to rebel. In fact, so ready were they to make war against their father that Louis was able to persuade them to swear an oath that they would not make peace with Henry II without Louis' permission.[2]

After two years of fighting, Henry and Louis tried to make peace, but Richard was still fighting in Poitou. Henry II marched south to meet Richard, but father and son never met in battle. Instead, Richard retreated, letting city after city fall to his father. On September 23, Richard, weeping, threw himself at his father's feet and begged for forgiveness. Henry pulled Richard to his feet and kissed him. The rebellion was over—at least for a while.

Henry and Eleanor

Henry and Eleanor were formidable characters, even by twelfth-century standards. Henry was one of the most powerful rulers in western Europe.[3] He was constantly on the move and took his entire court with him, which was a huge undertaking in those days. Contemporaries thought him handsome in a rugged sort of way. He was tall, had broad shoulders, and lots of red-gold hair. His temper was unpredictable, and he could be vindictive. Most of the time, he was patient and generous. He frequently gave alms to the poor, often in secret.[4] Henry was respectful of the clergy and established a number of churches and monasteries. In contrast to his energetic personality, he was intelligent and well educated. He spoke many languages, but French was his first language.

Henry II and Eleanor of Aquitaine's effigies in Fontevraud Abbey, France

Eleanor of Aquitaine was Henry's match in many ways, although we know less about her because she was a woman (and histories of women were rare in those days). She inherited most of southern France when her father died. She was ten years older than Henry, but beautiful and charming enough to captivate him. They married just two months after her first husband, Louis VII of France, divorced her for failing to give him a son. Henry was glad to get both her and her kingdom of Aquitaine.

Eleanor wasn't like most women of her era. Most likely, she married Henry for both love and money. She was a talented and capable woman of strong opinions, and she expressed them freely. Most heiresses were content to let their husbands control their property, but not Eleanor. She took an active role in running Aquitaine.

Besides meddling in politics, Eleanor is known for her influence in art, literature, and culture in general. Some historians credit her for the chivalrous version of King Arthur. Apparently, she and her daughter Marie hired writers to add stories of romance to the existing Arthur legend in order to promote ideals of courtly love. However, according to historian John Gillingham, there's no proof that either mother or daughter had anything to do with that version of King Arthur.[5]

Gustave Doré's *The Discovery of the True Cross* shows the knights' devotion to the holy relic. There's no way to prove or disprove that the cross the Christian knights carried into battle at the Horns of Hattin was truly the one on which Jesus died.

CHAPTER
THREE

RICHARD, DUKE OF NORMANDY

Henry II was generous with his rebellious sons. The old king reinstated their lands and titles. He also insisted that Richard restore the lands and castles of any baron who fought for Henry.[1] In addition, barons fighting for Richard had to give back the lands they had won on his behalf. Richard found himself at war with his own barons!

Richard was just twenty years old, but he met the challenge. Most castles he retook with little effort. However, Château de Taillebourg was protected on three sides by cliffs and on the fourth by triple walls and fortified towers.[2] No one had dared attack it—until Richard, that is. His men laid siege to the walled side. The defenders thought that eventually Richard would give up and go away, but he didn't. When Richard refused to leave, the knights of Taillebourg opened the gates and attacked Richard's men face to face. It was a mistake. They were no match for Richard's knights. Once inside the castle walls, Richard quickly took over.

Hearing news of Taillebourg, Richard's next opponent, Geoffrey of Rancon at Pons, surrendered. Richard succeeded in restoring his authority as the duke of Aquitaine. Commoners, at least, were grateful. As noted by Gerald of Wales, ". . . that hitherto untamed country . . . that he might quell the insubordination of an unruly people, and make innocence secure amongst evildoers."[3] In other words, Richard brought order to his kingdom, and protected the commoners from the greedy barons.

Richard seemed to have the upper hand, until his brother Geoffrey took advantage of a family Christmas celebration in 1182. Richard had built a castle on Geoffrey's land (or at least the land Geoffrey would inherit through his wife). To retaliate, Geoffrey sought the support of Richard's barons. Many were still angry with Richard for forcing them to give back lands they'd won during the rebellion a few years earlier. Geoffrey had no trouble gaining their support against Richard.

To please his father, Richard gave Geoffrey the castle, but that just made Geoffrey angrier. He demanded that Richard pay him homage. Geoffrey wanted Richard to admit that he was not his equal. Trying to settle the dispute, Henry II commanded both of his younger sons to pay homage to their elder brother, Henry. Richard refused because Aquitaine was independent. Because he had inherited Aquitaine from his mother, he believed his holdings were separate from his father's (and therefore also separate from his brothers').

Eventually, Richard agreed to his father's request, but he insisted that Henry acknowledge that he (Richard) and his heirs were the sole lords of Aquitaine. Henry angrily refused.

Richard really was the only truly independent ruler of the brothers. Henry and Geoffrey were jealous. Geoffrey incited Richard's barons to rebel. Henry joined Geoffrey's cause against Richard.

Hearing of the war, Henry II set out to meet his son Henry. He hoped to put an end to the conflict, once and for all. Near Limoges, some of young Henry's men attacked his father. Young Henry tried to make amends, but the old king was angry. Henry II joined Richard against his other sons.

Geoffrey and young Henry wanted Aquitaine, and if they couldn't have his land, they'd demand his fealty. Richard's rebelling barons wanted a duke they could manipulate, or at least ignore. Philip Augustus, the young king of France, was as meddlesome as Louis had been and sent mercenaries to help the rebels.[4]

Geoffrey, young Henry, the rebelling barons, and the French mercenaries showed no mercy to the villages of Aquitaine. Finally, fate stepped in. Young Henry fell ill with dysentery late in May 1183. He died in June before reconciling with his father. By the end of June, the rebellion was over.

When young Henry died, Richard became Henry II's apparent heir. He would become the king of England and the duke of Normandy and Anjou. Sharing the kingdom had failed before (with young Henry), so Henry II refused to make Richard a joint king. Instead, Richard would have to wait until his father died.

Henry II stipulated that Richard must give Aquitaine to John (the youngest brother) when he became king, but Richard refused. John was his father's favorite, but Richard saw him for what he was: a spoiled, indulged, and often cruel young man. Richard felt a responsibility to his people, and he feared John would abuse them.

When Richard defied his father and refused to give up his dukedom, the rebellion was on again. John and Geoffrey sent a large

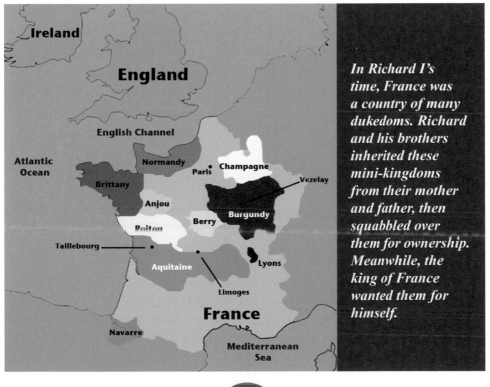

In Richard I's time, France was a country of many dukedoms. Richard and his brothers inherited these mini-kingdoms from their mother and father, then squabbled over them for ownership. Meanwhile, the king of France wanted them for himself.

band of mercenaries into Aquitaine in 1184. Richard retaliated by attacking Geoffrey's dukedom of Brittany.

Henry II summoned his sons to England, where they quarreled for the next few years. Only death brought them together again. In August 1186, Geoffrey died after a jousting accident. Philip, the king of France, claimed the dukedom as its overlord, essentially taking a large piece of Henry II's kingdom. With a common enemy (Philip), the Plantagenets stopped bickering among themselves, and together they took up arms against him.

Normandy, Anjou, and Aquitaine fought for Henry II. Paris, Burgundy, and Champagne joined Philip. Richard and Philip reached a truce, but Henry refused to accept Philip's terms. The two sides met at Berry in June 1187. Just before the battle, Henry sent Richard back to Philip asking for new terms. Kneeling before Philip, Richard offered the French king his sword and went a step further. He agreed to fight with Philip against his own father if the old king broke the truce.[5] Philip agreed.

Peace didn't last long. In November 1187, Richard heard the news of the battle at the Horns of Hattin. Muslims had destroyed the Christian army, massacred prisoners, taken Jerusalem's Christian king as prisoner, and taken most of the major cities, including Jerusalem. Perhaps the worst news was that the True Cross, the most sacred relic in all Christendom, was now in the hands of nonbelievers. The next morning, Richard took the Cross—a holy vow to go to the Holy Land on a new crusade.

Instead of being proud of Richard, Henry II and Philip were angry. To save face, they would have to go with him. Early in 1188, both kings reluctantly took the Cross and promised to join Richard on the crusade.

Before they could leave, Philip stirred the Plantagenet pot a bit by insisting that Henry recognize Richard as his heir. When Richard asked his father if he intended to comply, Henry refused to answer. It's unclear what motivated Henry to remain silent on the question of his heir. Richard responded to his father's silence by saying, "I have no choice but to believe the impossible to be true."[6] Richard knelt before

In 1860, Italian sculptor Baron Carlo Marochetti created the bronze equestrian statue **Richard I: Coeur de Lion** *(Lionheart), which stands in front of the Houses of Parliament in London. Scenes of Crusade life adorn the statue's pedestal.*

Philip and paid homage to him, in front of his father! W. L. Warren suggests that Henry's silence was only an attempt to keep Richard in line: "Henry had adopted the tactic of trying to discipline Richard by keeping him in uncertainty."[7]

Philip made more demands and Henry countered them, but still he refused to acknowledge Richard as his heir. That drove Richard toward Philip. After yet one more battle between them, Richard caught sight of his father trying to escape. Alone, unarmed, and wearing no armor, Richard rode after his father. Most likely, he hoped to capture him before any of Philip's men did.[8] One of Henry's men turned his horse and rode straight for Richard, with his lance ready for attack. Richard shouted at him, "God's feet, man, kill me not! I am

Third Crusade: Richard the Lionheart and Philip Augustus Take the Cross, *from a medieval manuscript. Richard I was a brilliant soldier. Philip II didn't share Richard's quest for battle. Had Richard not taken the cross, it is unlikely that Philip would have done so on his own.*

unarmed!"[9] Henry's man replied, "Let the devil kill you, for I will not."[10] Instead of killing Richard, he plunged his lance into Richard's horse, and Henry escaped to Chinon.

As a condition of Henry's surrender, he finally recognized Richard as his heir. The matter of Alice was finally dropped and Richard never married her. Sick and discouraged, Henry asked for a list of his nobles who had joined Richard and Philip's army. Seeing his favorite son John on the list broke his heart.[11] Henry II died three days later, on July 6, 1189.

As his father had been generous with him years before, King Richard I was generous with Henry's loyal nobles. He condemned Henry's deserters, but didn't punish them. To his brother John, he gave several counties in England and four thousand pounds a year.[12] Philip and Richard agreed to set out for the Third Crusade in spring of 1190.

Philip Augustus

Perhaps no one, other than his father, challenged Richard as much as Philip II of France. Philip conspired with Richard to defeat Henry II. While Richard was in the Holy Land, Philip ignored an oath and plundered Normandy.

Philip was short, stocky, and weak. He had no stomach for war and no mind for military strategy. In battle with Richard, Philip almost always retreated. In only one way did Philip outshine Richard—Philip was a better diplomat. However, Philip's diplomacy wasn't one of honor. He lied and deceived his opponents. Perhaps that was the only way Philip could compete with the formidable Richard.

Despite his shortcomings, history is kind to Philip. French historian Robert Fawtier described him as "the great king of the Capetian dynasty."[13] ("The Capetian dynasty" refers to the rulers of France from 987 to 1328, during the Middle Ages.) His kingdom included little more than the city of Paris when he became king. His authority was subject to the good will of his dukes, such as Richard.

Philip's goal was to conquer the French dukedoms held by the Plantagenets. Henry and Eleanor were both French by birth, and Eleanor's holdings, which she gave to Richard, included a large portion of southern France.

When Philip died, France was a strong and united country, having expanded twofold from his original kingdom. Just as important, he left France financially sound. Thanks to Philip, France was the richest and most powerful country in Europe during the thirteenth century, and England was one of the poorest and weakest.

Philip II of France—a copperplate engraving from 1793

The Coronation of Richard I in Westminster Abbey,
1189. According to court chronicler Roger of Hoveden,
four barons carried a silken canopy on four spears
for Richard (shown between the boy and the bishop).
Roger accompanied Richard on the Third Crusade. Most
likely, he was at Richard's coronation and shares a
truthful account of it.

RICHARD THE LIONHEART

After his coronation as the king of England, Richard prepared for the crusade, but he needed money. The royal treasury was empty. Henry II had levied the Saladin Tax shortly before his death to help pay for the previous crusade against Saladin, so a new tax was a bad idea. Besides, it would take too long to collect.

Instead of a new tax, Richard allowed those who had taken the Cross, but changed their minds, to buy their way out of the crusade. He also auctioned public offices and royal manors. (Purchasing a public office or title was common in those days.)

After making all his final preparations, Richard sailed to France, where he put his affairs in order. While there, he met with Sancho VI of Navarre and agreed to marry Sancho's daughter, Berengaria. Richard's mother, Eleanor, had chosen Berengaria for him: Her dowry was large enough to help Richard finance England's participation in the Third Crusade.

On June 27, Richard's army left for Vezelay, where he was to meet Philip. The town was too small for two huge armies, so the crusaders set up their tents outside the city walls. The surrounding countryside had to feed thousands of Richard's men.

During the first week of July, the two European kings led their armies toward Lyons. A bridge over the Rhône River collapsed, and it

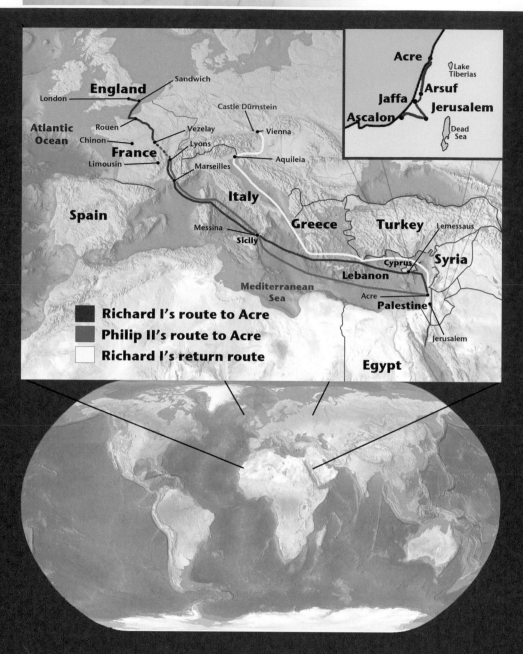

The route of Richard I's and Philip II's armies to Acre. Twice the armies split on their way to the Holy Land. After taking Acre, Richard marched south toward his main goal: Jerusalem. During his return to England, after what may have been a shipwreck in Aquileia, he traveled through Europe, in secret.

took three days to ferry the combined army across. Tens of thousands of men traveling together was proving to be impossible to manage, so the armies took different routes.

In September, Richard and Philip met again in Sicily. The combined army was more than the island could feed. The price of food and wine shot up. Tensions grew when the new king, Tancred of Lecce, refused to return Joan (Richard's newly widowed sister) and her dower to Richard. Unknown to Richard, Philip (supposedly) warned Tancred not to trust Richard. He even promised to help Tancred should he decide to attack Richard.

On October 3, a fight over a loaf of bread so enraged Richard that he captured Messina. The battle was over quickly. Tancred gave Joan and twenty thousand ounces of gold to Richard, who agreed to come to Tancred's aid if invaded. Richard shared the gold with Philip.

The peace didn't last long. Richard learned that Philip and Tancred had conspired against him, but Philip swore the letter was a fake. To appease Richard, Philip finally released him from his promise to marry Alice, which was good considering Richard was betrothed to Berengaria. It's doubtful that anyone really expected Richard to marry Alice. She had become Henry II's mistress!

Philip set sail for the Holy Land on March 30. Richard stayed behind to wait for his mother and Berengaria. On April 10, 1191, Richard, Joan, Berengaria, and the army followed Philip. (Eleanor returned to France. At seventy, she was too old for a crusade.) He had started his journey ten months earlier, but had truly just begun.

Richard's fleet of more than 200 ships was huge by twelfth-century standards. Each transport ship carried forty horses, forty knights (along with their arms and equipment), forty foot soldiers, fifteen sailors, and food for the men and horses for a year.[1]

After a short detour to capture Lemessus in Cyprus, Richard married Berengaria, on May 12. Then he conquered the whole island of Cyprus. When he was done, he set sail for the Holy Land on June 5.

Richard's army sailed into Acre early in June. The city was built on a small peninsula. The south and west sides were protected by sea walls and the Mediterranean Sea. Turreted walls fortified the two remaining sides.

King Philip's army was already camped outside the city walls, setting up siege engines, which were huge wooden catapult-type machines. The crusaders suffered from the heat and dust storms. Hot winds blew fine grit into their food, ears, teeth, noses, and eyes. Inside the city, Muslims shot arrows at the Christians. The stench from rotting corpses and animal and human waste fouled the air.

The inhabitants waited for Saladin to rescue them. Many times, Saladin's army attacked the Christians surrounding Acre, but the crusaders outnumbered Saladin's local troops. After two years of defending Acre from multiple crusading armies, the city agreed to the following terms of surrender, without Saladin's approval:

- To surrender the city immediately.
- To release fifteen hundred Christian prisoners.
- To pay the Christian kings two hundred thousand gold bezants.
- To return the True Cross to the Christians.[2]

In return, the Christian army promised to spare the lives of Acre's defending soldiers. They would keep the Muslims as prisoners until Saladin met their terms of surrender.

As usual, twelfth-century egos got in the way of the Christian celebration. Duke Leopold of Austria planted his banner beside those of Richard and Philip. He had no legal right to claim an equal share of the victory or the spoils—he wasn't on the same level as the two kings. Richard's men quickly tore down the banner and threw it into a ditch, which upset Leopold and set events into motion that would change Richard's history and perhaps even the history of England.

Saladin was shocked by the terms, when he learned of them, but the damage was done. All he could do was stall. Richard agreed to wait.

While Richard waited for Saladin's reply, Philip announced that he was going home. The English king begged Philip to stay, but Philip didn't have the heart or stomach for war. However, Philip did promise not to attack Richard's French lands while he was still crusading.

Richard faced a military dilemma when Saladin failed to meet the terms of surrender. While Richard waited at Acre, the Muslims were fortifying Jerusalem or perhaps even planning a counterattack against Acre. He couldn't leave several thousand Muslim prisoners behind. He couldn't spare the men to guard them, or the food to feed them.

Richard's solution was gruesome. Two thousand seven hundred prisoners were marched out of Acre in small groups and killed, within full view of Saladin's camp. Saladin was powerless to rescue them.

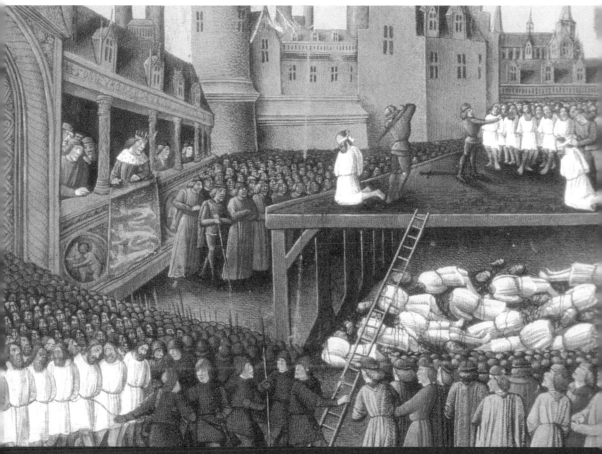

After the battle of Acre, Richard I had 2,700 Muslim prisoners put to death when Saladin refused to meet his terms of surrender.

It's important to view this event within the emotions and expectations of the twelfth century. In modern times, Richard's decision would be unthinkable. On the other hand, his contemporaries remembered that Saladin had massacred all the captive Christian knights after the battle of Hattin a few years earlier. No one condemned Saladin. No one condemned Richard.[3]

Richard was a brilliant commander and fierce in battle. His honor and skill earned him the nickname Lionheart. We don't know who first used the name or when, but certainly it was while he lived. Richard was a legend in his own time.

Parts of the ancient walls of Acre still stand between the city and the Mediterranean Sea. The waves and the weather continue to erode them.

Concerning Crusaders Who Were to Travel by Sea

Richard spent many months preparing for the journey to the Middle East to free Jerusalem from the Muslims. While in Chinon (a town in France), he negotiated his marriage to Berengaria of Navarre. One of his final tasks was to issue a set of regulations for the long voyage to the Holy Land:

- Any man who kills another, shall be bound to the dead man and, if at sea, be thrown overboard, if on land, buried with him.
- If it be proved by lawful witnesses that any man has drawn his knife on another, or has struck him and drawn blood, his hand shall be cut off.
- If any man strikes another without drawing blood, he shall be ducked in the sea three times.
- Swearing at another man shall be punished by a fine.
- A man convicted of theft shall be shaved like a champion, tarred and feathered, and set ashore at the first landfall.[4]

By today's standards, Richard's punishments seem barbaric. In fact, some historians use these laws to support their claims that Richard was a brutal man and a ruthless leader. His laws were indeed harsh, but we must judge Richard and these laws within the context of his time and his quest. Much of the voyage was made by ship, where conditions where crowded. These men were all knights and warriors; they were headed to war and perhaps even death. The trip would be worse than tense. At any given moment, war was likely to break out within his own ranks. The only way Richard could hope to control such a large group of volatile men was to make the punishments so severe that no one would dare to break the peace.

As Richard I led his soldiers into battle at Jaffa, he is said to have cheered, "Cursed forever be he who follows me not!"

For Your Info

Detail of crusaders from "Overseas Voyages," a manuscript illuminated by Sebastian Marmoret (c. 1490). Muslim soldiers wore only light body armor and chain mail. Many of the Christians removed their heavy body armor in the heat. Often, tunics were the only way to identify Christians from Muslims.

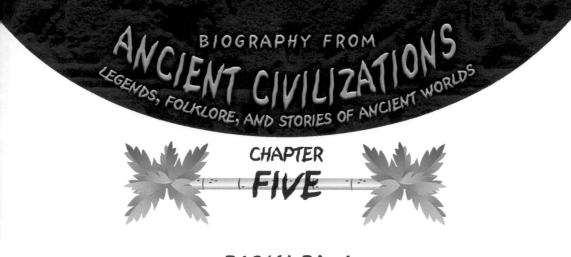
CHAPTER

FIVE

RICHARD I

The Christian army left Acre two days later, on August 22. Instead of marching directly to Jerusalem, they headed south toward Jaffa, because the sea would protect them on one side. The route was flat, which would leave them less vulnerable to an ambush.

The heat was relentless, and the men baked inside their armor and leather. They carried from fifty to eighty pounds of gear on their backs.[1] Removing their protective gear was too risky: Saladin's cavalry attacked several times. Their only protection was to keep marching, and that's what they did, through the heat and Muslim arrows. They didn't even stop to bury their dead. The wounded forced themselves to continue marching, despite their pain. For most, however, the protective gear did its job. Soldiers walked with dozens of arrows embedded in their leather—the arrows stopped at the chain mail beneath their leather coverings. Even the Muslims were impressed, as noted by Beha ed-Din: "One cannot help admiring the wonderful patience displayed by these people. I saw some Frankish foot soldiers with from one to ten arrows sticking into them, and still advancing at their usual pace without leaving the ranks."[2]

On September 1, they emerged from the Forest of Arsuf onto an open plain to find Saladin's army "as thick as drops of rain."[3] Once again, Richard's military expertise saved him. He divided his army into five divisions before Saladin's cavalry bore down on them, crying, *"Allah akhbar!"*[4] (God is great).

For hours, Richard's army marched on, under continuous attack. Knights kept the rear so tight that Saladin's men couldn't break their ranks. In the afternoon heat, a knight named Baldwin le Caron finally broke ranks and drove his horse toward the enemy. Other knights soon followed. Richard couldn't recall his men, so he ordered an all-out attack. The Christian army fell with full force on the Muslims, sending them into chaos. Saladin tried to recover his men, but in the end, he retreated. Saladin lost a lot of soldiers that day, and his military reputation suffered a major blow.

Richard found Jaffa in ruins. His army spent September and October rebuilding it. From Jaffa, Richard wrote to Saladin suggesting peace terms. In return for taking his army home, Richard asked for the city of Jerusalem and the return of the True Cross. Saladin refused both requests.

Richard offered to marry his sister Joan to Saladin's brother, Safadin, the lord of Palestine. Joan's dowry would include all the coastal towns Richard had captured, and the couple would rule Jerusalem together.

Saladin didn't believe Richard. Joan would never agree to marry a Muslim. No one really knows if Richard ever intended to keep the terms. Most likely, Richard was stalling for time. When Saladin accepted his terms, Richard reneged, saying his sister refused to marry an infidel (non-Christian). He suggested that Safadin convert to Christianity. They both gained a little time from the farce, but that's all.

Toward the end of October, Richard marched his army inland. Along the route to Jerusalem they found castle after castle destroyed. Richard's army stopped long enough to rebuild these fortresses. By the end of November they were only halfway to Jerusalem. Continuous rain soaked the men and their gear. Food mildewed. The promise of Jerusalem kept them going.

However, Richard knew something his troops did not. Even if Jerusalem fell to the crusaders, Richard knew that at least half of his army would go home after that battle. He couldn't defend and hold the city against counterattacks with half his army. Nor could he supply the city, since Saladin's army was between Jerusalem and the ports. Jerusalem was a hopeless cause for now. On January 10, 1192, Richard gave the order to retreat for the winter. His men were shattered.[5] Richard was "worn out with grief and toil such as no tongue nor pen can describe."[6]

Richard spent that winter and spring in Ascalon, east of Jerusalem, on the coast. In early June, he again led his army inland. From Montjoie, he and his men got their first glimpse of the Holy City. It would be Richard's one and only sighting. Nothing had changed from the previous fall. Saladin had poisoned the wells outside the city. There was little hope of taking Jerusalem quickly, and with no water, a long siege was out of the question.

Inside Jerusalem, Saladin also worried. Richard had already humiliated him twice. Malek Rik frightened Saladin's emirs so much that they were ready to surrender.[7] Saladin knew he risked everything by staying. Of course, neither leader knew the other was worried.

Richard retreated to Acre and started negotiations for peace. The two men still couldn't agree on terms and met in battle at Jaffa. Richard, for a third time, was the victor.

In late August, the enemies finally reached a truce. Muslims would control Jerusalem, but Christian pilgrims could visit, and all Christian cities would remain Christian. The truce would last three years (some sources say five years). Signed on September 2, 1192, the truce officially ended the Third Crusade.

Richard left for home on October 9. Saladin went to Damascus, but was dead within a few months. He rode out on a bitterly cold day to greet pilgrims returning home from Mecca. That evening, he had a fever and never recovered. He died on March 3, 1193.

Richard's journey home took him through Leopold's dukedom. Because Richard's men had offended the duke by removing his banner at Acre, they traveled in disguise, as pilgrims. Pilgrims had the pope's protection, but respect for the pope's orders didn't protect Richard from Leopold.

Richard was held for ransom in Castle Dürnstein, which overlooked the Danube River in Austria. The castle was nearly destroyed in 1646 by the Swedes. The ruins are now a popular tourist attraction.

One traditional story claims that Richard was captured outside Vienna, Austria, dressed as a cook while stirring a pot. Apparently, the huge ruby ring on his finger gave him away. Leopold was thrilled, as were Philip of France and John in England. Pope Celestine III excommunicated Leopold for kidnapping Richard.

Emperor Henry VI of the Holy Roman Empire purchased Richard and promptly put him on trial for war crimes. Richard defended himself well, according to the contemporary court poet William the Breton: "When Richard replied, he spoke so eloquently and regally, in so lion-hearted a manner, that it was as though he had forgotten where he was and the undignified circumstances in which he had been captured, and imagined himself to be seated on the throne of his ancestors."[8] After he spoke, the assembly burst into applause and acquitted him, unanimously.

Despite the verdict, Richard still wasn't free to leave. It took Eleanor, Richard's mother, several months to collect the ransom of 100,000 marks of silver. A 25 percent tax was levied on income and property. The monasteries were forced to hand over land, and churches gave gilded treasure. The outrageous amount devastated England financially.

When Richard was finally released, Philip of France reportedly sent John a letter, saying, "Look to yourself; the devil is unbound."[9] Richard and Eleanor landed in Sandwich on March 13, 1194. The first thing Richard had to do was reclaim several cities from John. Most of John's holdings immediately surrendered, but Richard was forced into battle at Nottingham. When Richard hanged a few captured prisoners, the city surrendered.

As the king of England, Richard spent only six months of his reign in England.[10] In May, he sailed to Normandy (in France). There, John begged his brother for mercy. Richard forgave him.

Philip of France had also been busy in Richard's absence and, despite his promise not to attack, held many of Richard's cities. Within a month, Richard had recovered several of his southern castles. For nearly five years, the two kings waged battles and signed peace treaties.

On March 26, 1199, Richard's men attacked the castle of Châlus-Chabrol in Limousin. Richard arrived, wearing no armor. Only one enemy knight, wielding a frying pan as a shield (according to the traditional story) was defending the walls. Richard applauded the knight's bravery, and the knight shot him in the neck with his crossbow.

A doctor cut out the iron bolt and bandaged Richard's wound. Within a few days the wound was infected. Gangrene set in and spread. Richard summoned Eleanor and asked to see the knight who shot him. Richard forgave him, said confession, and died. It was April 6, 1199.

John was now king, and England would barely survive him.

Richard I was buried at Fontevraud Abbey in a tomb at his father's feet. His heart was sent to Rouen Cathedral. During the French revolution, it was discarded as rubbish.

Some modern historians condemn Richard I because they judge him by modern standards instead of viewing his life through twelfth-century values. In Richard's England, faith and courage were admired above all else.[11] Richard's contemporaries saw him as honorable, generous, noble, and courteous.[12] His feats of courage in battle are to this day considered extraordinary. He was a brilliant soldier and military strategist. Leading every battle, he won the respect and admiration of even his enemies. He earned the name Richard the Lionheart.

King John and the Magna Carta

After Richard's death, John was crowned King of England on May 27, 1199. John subsequently lost all of the Plantagenet holdings in France, except for Gascony. His continuous wars with Philip bankrupted the country. He is infamous for treating his subjects so badly that his barons rebelled. In June 1215, they forced him to sign the Magna Carta, the Great Charter.

Technically, the Magna Carta was a peace treaty between John and his barons. It established rights for men and limited the power of the king. Initially, these rights were granted just to the barons. Eventually, these rights spread from the barons through the upper levels of society. The Magna Carta gave all free men the right and responsibility to bear arms, something only the nobility had previously had. In addition, the king could not levy taxes without permission from the leading churchmen and barons. Restrictions on royal officials, particularly sheriffs, curtailed their abuse. Perhaps most important, the charter established trial by jury. A king no longer could imprison a person or confiscate lands on a whim.

A colored wood engraving of King John signing the Magna Carta in 1215, Runnymede, England

John died the next year, in October 1216, most likely from dysentery, complicated by overindulgence.[13]

Photograph of the Magna Carta

History casts John as the villain in the Plantagenet play. He conspired against his father, tried to usurp his brother's crown, and, by tradition, murdered his nephew, Prince Arthur, who had a legitimate claim to the throne.[14] He taxed the people mercilessly, giving rise to the legendary folk hero Robin Hood of Nottingham. John was feared by many, but few if any admired or loved him. As noted by a contemporary chronicler named Barnwell: "at his end, few mourned for him."[15]

CHAPTER NOTES

Chapter One. A Holy War

1. Antony Bridge, *Richard the Lionheart* (New York: Grafton Books, 1989), p. 172.
2. Ibid., p. 176.
3. Ibid.
4. Ibid.
5. Ibid.
6. Stanley Lane-Poole, *Saladin and the Fall of Jerusalem* (Mechanicsburg, Pennsylvania: Greenhill Books, 2002), p. 110.
7. Helen Nicholson and David Nicolle, *God's Warriors: Crusaders, Saracens and the Battle for Jerusalem* (University Park, Illinois: Osprey Publishing, 2005), p. 16.

Chapter Two. A Twelfth-Century Prince

1. Antony Bridge, *Richard the Lionheart* (New York: Grafton Books, 1989), p. 10.
2. John Gillingham, *Richard the Lionheart* (New York: Times Books, 1978), p. 66.
3. Elizabeth Hallam, General Editor, *The Plantagenet Chronicles* (New York: Crescent Books, 1995), p. 94.
4. Ibid.
5. Gillingham, pp. 59–62.

Chapter Three. Richard, Duke of Normandy

1. John Gillingham, *Richard the Lionheart* (New York: Times Books, 1978), p. 70.
2. Antony Bridge, *Richard the Lionheart* (New York: Grafton Books, 1989), p. 61.
3. Ibid., p. 58.
4. Ibid., p. 76.
5. Ibid., p. 89.
6. Gillingham, p. 120.
7. Ibid., p. 121.
8. Bridge, p. 98.

9. Ibid.
10. Ibid.
11. Gillingham, p. 124.
12. Bridge, p. 104.
13. Elizabeth Hallam, General Editor, *The Plantagenet Chronicles* (New York: Crescent Books, 1995), p. 205.

Chapter Four. Richard the Lionheart

1. Antony Bridge, *Richard the Lionheart* (New York: Grafton Books, 1989), p. 136.
2. John Gillingham, *Richard the Lionheart* (New York: Times Books, 1978), p. 176.
3. Bridge, p. 161.
4. Ibid., p. 118–119.

Chapter Five: Richard I

1. Antony Bridge, *Richard the Lionheart* (New York: Grafton Books, 1989), p. 165.
2. Ibid., p. 166.
3. Ibid., p. 167.
4. Ibid.
5. John Gillingham, *Richard the Lionheart* (New York: Times Books, 1978), p. 200.
6. Bridge, p. 177.
7. Gillingham, p. 211.
8. Bridge, pp. 201–202.
9. Ibid., p. 208.
10. Nigel Blundell and Kate Farrington, *Ancient England* (Edison, New Jersey: Chartwell Books, Inc., 1996), p. 68.
11. Bridge, p. 249.
12. Ibid., p. 242.
13. Elizabeth Hallam, General Editor, *The Plantagenet Chronicles* (New York: Crescent Books, 1995), p. 321.
14. Blundell and Farrington, p. 70.
15. Hallam, p. 265.

1157 Richard is born on September 8 to Henry II and Eleanor of Aquitaine.

1168 Richard moves to Aquitaine with his mother.

1172 Henry II names Richard the duke of Aquitaine but retains the power behind the title.

1173 Richard asserts his claim to Aquitaine by rebelling.

1174 Henry II defeats Richard, then pardons him on September 23.

1183 Young Henry (Richard's eldest brother) dies. Richard becomes heir apparent to his father's titles, including King of England.

1186 Geoffrey (Richard's elder brother) dies after being wounded in a jousting tournament.

1187 Richard takes the Cross in November.

1189 Henry II dies on July 6, and Richard succeeds his father as king of England. Richard is crowned on September 3.

1190 Richard leaves for the Holy Lands.

1191 Richard captures Cyprus in May. He marries Berengaria of Navarre in May. He arrives in Acre on June 6. Muslim-held Acre surrenders to the crusaders on July 12. Philip II leaves the Crusade for home in August. Richard slaughters 2,700 Muslim prisoners at Acre in August. He wins the battle of Arsuf on September 7.

1192 Richard withdraws to Jaffa and then to Acre in July, instead of attacking Jerusalem. He wins the battle for Jaffa in August. Richard and Saladin reach a truce in September. Richard starts for home on October 9. He is taken prisoner in Austria and held for ransom in December.

1194 Emperor Henry VI releases Richard on February 4, after Eleanor pays his ransom. Richard and Eleanor arrive in England on March 13. Richard leaves England for France.

1199 Richard is wounded on March 26 by an arrow from a crossbow. He dies on April 6 from infection in the wound. His younger brother, John, becomes king of England.

1066	William the Conqueror defeats the English at the battle of Hastings and becomes the first Norman (French) king of England.
1095	Pope Urban II gives a speech urging a crusade.
1096	The Peasants (or Paupers) Crusade fails.
1097	The Knights Crusade begins. It will become known as the First Crusade.
1099	Crusaders capture Jerusalem on July 15.
1120	Order of the Knights Templar is founded. About 300 people, including several French and English nobles, die in the *White Ship* tragedy.
1137/38	Saladin is born.
1139	Civil War in England begins between Stephen and Matilda.
1144	Muslims recapture Christian strongholds along the land route to Jerusalem.
1145	The Second Crusade is launched. It lasts until 1149.
1152	King Louis VII divorces Eleanor of Aquitaine. Eleanor of Aquitaine marries Henry Plantagenet.
1153	Crusaders under Baldwin III capture the port of Ascalon near Jerusalem. English Civil War ends.
1154	Henry Plantagenet becomes Henry II, King of England, after Stephen dies.
1174	Saladin becomes leader of Egypt and Damascus.
1185	King Baldwin of Jerusalem dies, and Guy of Lusignan succeeds him.
1187	Saladin declares jihad against the crusaders. His army wins the battle of Hattin on July 4. Jerusalem falls to Saladin.
1189	The Third Crusade is launched to reclaim Jerusalem.
1193	Six months after the Third Crusade ends, Saladin dies (March).
1202	The Fourth Crusade begins.
1204	Eleanor of Aquitaine dies and is buried with Henry II and Richard I at the Abbey of Fontevraud. The Fourth Crusade sacks Constantinople.
1212	The Children's Crusade fails to reach the Holy Land.
1215	King John signs the Magna Carta.
1216	King John dies. His son Henry III becomes king of England.
1219	The Fifth Crusade (1218–1221) occupies Damietta, Egypt.
1223	Philip II, king of France, dies.
1229	The Sixth Crusade (1228–1229) briefly holds Jerusalem.
1244	The Saracens retake Jerusalem.
1248	The Seventh Crusade begins under King Louis IX of France; it ends in 1254.
1250	King Louis' army is defeated at the battle of Al Mansurah.
1270	The Eighth Crusade (1270–1272) attacks Tunisia.
1291	Acre, the last Christian fortress in the Holy Land, falls.

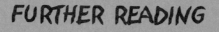

FURTHER READING

Books

Crompton, Samuel Willard. *The Third Crusade: Richard the Lionhearted vs. Saladin.* Philadelphia: Chelsea House Publishers, 2004.

Doherty, Katherine M., and Craig A. Doherty. *King Richard the Lionhearted and the Crusades in World History.* Berkley Heights, New Jersey: Enslow Publishing, Inc., 2002.

Gravett, Christopher. *Knight.* New York: DK Children, 2007.

Langley, Andrew. *Medieval Life.* New York: DK Children, 2004.

West, David, and Jackie Gaff. *Richard the Lionheart: The Life of a King and Crusader.* New York: The Rosen Publishing Group, Inc., 2005.

Worth, Richard. *Saladin: Sultan of Egypt and Syria.* Berkeley Heights, New Jersey: Enslow Publishers, Inc., 2007.

Works Consulted

Armstrong, Karen. *Holy War.* New York: Anchor Books, 2001.

Blundell, Nigel, and Kate Farrington. *Ancient England.* Edison, New Jersey: Chartwell Books, Inc., 1996.

Bridge, Antony. *Richard the Lionheart.* New York: M. Evans & Company, Inc., 1989.

Carpenter, David. *The Struggle for Mastery: Britain 1066–1284.* Oxford, England: Oxford University Press, 2003.

Gillingham, John. *Richard the Lionheart.* New York: Times Books, 1978.

Edbury, Peter W. *The Conquest of Jerusalem and the Third Crusade.* Hampshire, England: Ashgate Publishing, Ltd., 1998.

Hallam, Elizabeth, General Editor. *The Plantagenet Chronicles.* New York: Crescent Books, 1995.

Lane-Poole, Stanley. *Saladin and the Fall of Jerusalem.* Mechanicsburg, Pennsylvania: Greenhill Books, 2002.

Miller, David. *Richard the Lionheart: The Mighty Crusader.* London: The Orion Publishing Group, Ltd., 2003.

Nicholson, Helen, and David Nicolle. *God's Warriors: Crusaders, Saracens and the Battle for Jerusalem.* University Park, Illinois: Osprey Publishing, 2005.

Oldenbourg, Zoe. *The Crusades.* New York: Pantheon Books, 1966.

Ramsay, John H. *The Angevin Empire: Or the Three Reigns of Henry, Richard I, and John.* New York: MacMillan Co. 1903.

Reston, James, Jr. *Warriors of God.* New York: Doubleday, 2001.

Southern, R.W. *The Making of the Middle Ages.* New Haven, Connecticut: Yale University Press, 1953.

Turner, Ralph V., and Richard R. Heiser. *The Reign of Richard the Lionheart.* Harlow: England: Longman, an imprint of Pearson Education, 2000.

On the Internet

Arizona Center for Medieval and Renaissance Studies http://asu.edu/clas/acmrs/index.html

EyewitnessToHistory.com: Richard the Lionheart Massacres the Saracens http://www.eyewitnesstohistory.com/lionheart.htm

EyewitnessToHistory.com: The Crusaders Capture Jerusalem http://www.eyewitnesstohistory.com/crusades.htm

The Crusades http://crusades.boisestate.edu/

The Crusades http://pages.usherbrooke.ca/croisades/crusades.htm

The Knights Templar: A King Is Born http://www.templarhistory.com/richard.html

Medieval Crusades http://www.medievalcrusades.com/

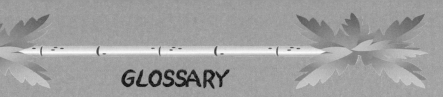

GLOSSARY

alliance (uh-LY-unts)—A formal agreement to cooperate.

betrothal (bee-TROH-thul)—A binding agreement to marry.

caravan (KAYR-uh-van)—A group of merchants traveling together for safety, usually in the Middle East and Asia.

crucified (KROO-sih-fyd)—To put to death by nailing or tying the hands and feet to a cross.

diplomacy (dih-PLOH-muh-see)—Using speech and compromise instead of violence in an attempt to solve political problems.

dower (DOW-er)—The portion of a deceased husband's estate that goes to his widow.

dukedom (DOOK-dum)—The territory ruled by a duke or duchess.

dysentery (DIS-in-tayr-ee)—An infectious disease of the bowel.

emir (ee-MEER)—A chieftain, prince, or commander in an Islamic country.

fealty (FEE-ul-tee)—The obligation to be faithful to a specific lord.

feudal vassal (FYOO-dul VAH-sul)— Someone who owes loyalty and service to a lord or rule by feudal law.

homage (AH-muj)—The ceremony whereby a lord's vassal kneels before him and swears allegiance.

infidel (IN-fuh-del)—The term Christians used for people who did not worship the Christian God.

inherit (in-HAYR-it)—To receive possessions, usually after the owner's death.

Kurd—An Islamic person living in Kurdistan.

mercenary (MER-sih-nayr-ee)—A soldier who fights for money or the love of war.

Muslim (MUZ-lum)—A follower of the religion Islam.

Norman (NOR-man)—A person from Normandy (northern France).

peasant (PEH-zant)—A member of the poorest class of people.

ransom (RAN-sum)—A payment made for the release of a captive.

renege (ree-NEG)—Change your mind; go back on your word.

Saracen (SAH-rah-sen)—A term used by crusaders to describe all Muslims in the Holy Land.

siege (SEEJ)—Surround a town or castle to cut off supplies and wage battle.

thatch (THATCH)—Dried grass.

truce (TROOS)—An agreement between two enemies to stop fighting, at least temporarily.

INDEX

Acre, battle of 9–10, 31–34, 37
Adela 15, 16
Alice 16, 26, 31
Arsuf 30, 37–38
Ascalon 39
Baldwin IV (the Leper), king of Jerusalem 7, 11
Baldwin le Caron 38
Berengaria 29, 31, 35
Brittany 17, 23, 24
Capetian dynasty 16, 17, 27
Castle of Chalûs-Chabrol 41
Celestine III, Pope 40
Constance 17
Dürnstein Castle 40
Eleanor of Aquitaine 13, 15, 16, 17, 18, 19, 27, 29, 31, 40, 41
Fontevraud Abbey 12, 19, 41
Fulk V, king of Jerusalem 15
Geoffrey V 15, 16
Geoffrey VI (see Plantagenet, Geoffrey)
Geoffrey of Rancon 21
Guy of Lusignan, king of Jerusalem 7, 8, 11, 24
Hattin (Horns of), battle of 8, 24, 34
Henry I, king of England 14, 15
Henry II, king of England (see also Henry of Anjou) 13, 15, 16, 17, 18, 19, 21, 22, 23–26, 27, 29, 31
Henry III (see Henry Plantagenet)
Henry VI, Emperor of the Holy Roman Empire 40
Henry of Anjou (see Henry II)
Hodierna (nurse) 15
Jaffa, battle of 35, 37, 38, 39
Jerusalem, battles of 7–10, 11, 15, 24, 33, 35, 38, 39
John Lackland, king of England 16, 18, 23–24, 26, 40, 41, 42
Lake Tiberias (Sea of Galilee) 8
Lemessus 6, 31
Leopold, duke of Austria 32, 39–40
Louis VII, king of France 16, 17, 18, 19, 22
Magna Carta 42

medieval lifestyle 13–14
Normandy 16, 23, 24, 25, 26, 41
Philip II (Philip Augustus), king of France 14, 22, 24, 25, 26, 27, 29, 30, 31, 32–33, 40, 41
Plantagenet, Geoffrey 16, 17, 18, 21, 22, 23–24
Plantagenet, Henry (the Young) 13, 16–17, 18, 22, 23
Plantagenet, Joan 16, 31, 38
Plantagenet, John (see John Lackland)
Plantagenet, Matilda (mother) 14–15, 16
Plantagenet, Matilda (sister) 16
Plantagenet, Richard (Richard the Lionheart)
    and Aquitaine 16, 21, 22, 23–24
    birth of 13
    childhood of 13–16, 18
    coronation of 28, 29
    as crusader 9–10, 24–25, 29–34, 35, 36, 37–39
    death of 41
    education of 16, 18
    family tree of 15–16
    as hostage 39–40
    marriage of 31
    route to Holy Land 29, 30, 31, 35, 37–39
Reginald (Raynald) of Châtillon 7, 8–9, 11
Robert of Gloucester 16
Roger of Hoveden 28
Safadin 38
Saladin (Salah ad-Din) 7–10, 11, 13, 29, 32–33, 34, 37–39
Sancho VI of Navarre 29
Second Crusade 7, 11
Stephen of Blois 15, 16
Taillebourg, battle of 21
Tancred of Lecce 31
Third Crusade 9–10, 11, 26, 28, 29–34, 35, 36, 37–39
True Cross 8, 20, 24, 32, 38
White Ship tragedy 15